Honey and Darkness

Honey and Darkness

Bill Poppen

Terri Verrette

with

Sarah Sydney Nash

Mary Elizabeth Thompson

Dan Tharp

M. Merrill

Kevin Urenda

Paulette Mauceri

Beth Anne Cox

Sandra Erickson

all photos by Bill Poppen

iUniverse, Inc.
New York   Bloomington

Honey and Darkness

iUniverse books may be ordered through booksellers or by contacting:

iUniverse
1663 Liberty Drive
Bloomington, IN 47403
www.iuniverse.com
1-800-Authors (1-800-288-4677)

ISBN: 978-1-4401-8186-3 (sc)
ISBN: 978-1-4401-8187-0 (ebk)

Printed in the United States of America

iUniverse rev. date: 10/7/2009

Contents

Preface:

Bill Poppen is well known in the online Xanga community as a poet of uncommon empathy and understanding. His poems elicit not only admiring comments, but also the recognition that comes from the clarity with which he describes emotions and circumstances we've all lived.

When Bill sent the invitation to join him in creating this collection, it was with excitement and humility that I and so many others answered his call. Through many voices of all ages, geographical locations, and life circumstances, Bill illuminates here the experience and perceptions of women.

Thank you, Bill, for your passion and your nurturing spirit. I'm proud to be your friend.

Terri Verrette

I met Terri Verrette on the internet by reading her blog. I was immediately impressed with her writing, especially her poems. *Hidden in Plain Sight* published by *ShadowPoetry* (www.shadowpoetry.com) in 2006, is filled with powerful and personal works especially for someone's first collection. Terri is a mother of two fine boys and has honed her skill by frequent posting and participation in writing workshops. Her poem, *Self Expression* ends with a most appropriate line, "I'm something else." I am most pleased that she agreed to work with me on this project. Without her effort, this work would not have been finished. Thanks Terri.

I also want to thank John C. Mannone for his editing and assistance with this project.

Photos, including the front and back covers are original photography by Bill Poppen.

Bill Poppen

Honey and Darkness
Bill Poppen

A coin has two sides:
one, copper bright,
reflecting honey-lit tones,
the other, dark,
hiding under shadow.

A woman, too:
honey-flecked side,
shadows drape her back.

I walk near her, keen to her scent.
Darkness and honey, mingling
bouquet of a woman.

Skin Talk

Terri Verrette

Side by side, legs atangle
pushing back so
older eyes can focus.
Waves of expression
rise above the pillow.

I want to tell you something true.
So true it will break. I want to
tell you something real.
So real it will burn. I want to
tell you something holy.
So holy it will live long
after I have gone.

But I'm busy
noticing your skin
and the gleam of light
from the curl of beard
below your ear.

Cloud Busting
Sarah Sydney Nash

I've spent the entire day escaping the inevitable.
Not avoiding it, as some might do.
I made random left turns, impulsive u-turns,
ran stop signs, drove back alleys
(doors unlocked, windows down).
I flashed a flagger, floored the gas at yellow warnings,
all of this and more, without fastening my seatbelt.
I've spent the entire day storm chasing
across the desert.
One foot precariously propped on my dash,
one elbow sun baking while dangling at the window,
one hand on the wheel,
one eye on the road,
and one eye on the forever sky.
Plump, warm raindrops baptized my windshield
just as I nearly surrendered to suffocating
midday heat.
Their splat sound broke the terminal silence
of wheels on road
white noise.
I witnessed the flap swish of wipers on glass,
grateful for smeared bug guts,
broken wings.
You can laugh out loud
for a long time
when you are alone.

Maiden Maelstrom
Sarah Sydney Nash

Shall I wear my hair long
or gathered into a bun
at the base of my neck
where the lips of men
once ruled my world?
Shall I use the same boxed color
on my hair? That color of sunshine,
of languid summer days.
Perhaps I should allow oak tree passages
lit by dappled breeze
and silver mosaic patterned natural
giddiness thrive?
Shall I let the tresses flow
around my shoulders
across my breasts,
a bright halo dancing
with strands of gold
against tips of rose?
Or maybe I'll slice the bits
of my history at my chin?
Shall I bundle up the curls
newborn hands tugged
while nursing
or ignore the spirals of
wheat colored memories?

Shall I leave Maiden
and embrace Mother,
while I accept those
threads of Crone
in my roots?

Silver

Mary Elizabeth Thompson

I see myself in you
through a pane of glass
always second
behind useless gold
we reflect, conduct, photograph
and kill germs
yet we aren't the most prized
Tin, Aluminum, and Chrome
imitate, but none do
as much,
as well,
only more cheaply

Devastation
Bill Poppen

She lets him walk away
without protest
amid yesterday's hail and rain.
He will not return.

She scrapes paint from her art cloth,
her pride, too.
Disfigures months of effort.
Brushes canvas with oils,
and beads of sweat with passion.
Demolishes her creation.
Frayed strings warp and twist.
Ravished hemp will hide
her strokes of beauty?

Her grand exhibit, devastated.
No rebirth lingers on her easel
shattering any future with him.

Sweet Surrender
Dan Tharp

Soft winds blow
echoes of my loneliness
across your face;
traces of love
and lust strewn haphazardly
amid lines --
crossed in moments
of passion.

Were there a single drop
of rain
to reclaim parched voids --
it was found
in the downpour
of requited love
exquisitely lavished
in moments
of sweet surrender.

Scent of Dawn
Dan Tharp

I watch the sun
    lick morning clouds;
    ascend the eastern horizon.

His light explodes
    upon her slopes,
    catching the scent of dawn...

morning mist
    and trickling streams
    mingle in their passions;

honey bees
    on wild flowers
    nectar to be taken.

Going Home
Mary Elizabeth Thompson

At dusk, I trudge the forest path while trees
lean over me like taskmasters, their bare branches,
whips poised against gray-dimmed sky.

Behind my time, too long a nap, too long
beside the singing brook, the sleeping stones
caressed into dreams of skipping.

As froth on the waves of time - that slippery fish -
my own sad dreams, abandoned hopes, skim
the groggy afternoon. Hurry now, as darkness

sprinkles the woods with shadows. Birds screech:
a carcass over here - termites over there -
and *soon-to-be a fallen traveler late*

going home.

A Red Scarf in Church
Terri Verrette

Slitted eyes peek
during prayer while
the preacher drones on
on to next Sunday's outline.
Red silk resting on
Maria's calf moves
like the breath of God
stroking, soothing
warming to the one opportunity
for open communion, partaken
in public, consumed
in private, still
some preacher somewhere drones
some parishioner somewhere wishes
the silk higher, to Maria's thigh.

Tattoos on Her Soul
Bill Poppen

William Blake's *Songs of Innocence*
shows ruffled pages, bent corners, side notes.
Chamomile tea spilled on them.

She devours words of passion,
settles into conversations with Blake, with God,
wishing for a time when she rode her bike
along Ten Mile Creek, hiked Abram's Falls,
when seduction was a word in Webster's.

A rumpled prayer rug rests beside her
walking stick and hiking boots. She longs
for new tattoos inked on her soul, indelible
marks that will not fade to pale.

Skydiving
Bill Poppen

She dreams
of skydiving in a Kimono
and walking fashion runways.
No Kimono hangs in her closet; never
strutted New York's garment district.

Each day perceives her imperfections
while standing in front of her full-length mirror.
Each misplaced mole or cellulite pleads
for an audience. Friends don't notice.
She hides what she can of each mark.

Co-workers notice her post-it-note
on her cubicle wall: "Intelligent, perfect women
skydive in Kimonos
and walk on fashion runways."

West Texas Homestead
Bill Poppen

He stands before her
as surveying a Renoir, overwhelmed
by red splashes from her nails, her lips.
He's entranced by her sparkling blue eyes,
her hair swept across her shoulders,
its crackle, as wind blown fields of barley.
Her words cool him as though dipped
in Box Elder Creek.
Her moves have grace of cirrus skies.

He thinks this is her settling place
fit to build a homestead.

Silent Song
Bill Poppen

No one can touch
what I want to feel.
No glance sends
vibrations into her soul.

No one, not God,
not even the Devil,
plays her strings,
making melodies of love.

Empty Cards
Bill Poppen

Frazzled hair, bloodshot eyes
and empty cards without answers
tell of her search.

Tabs of blue
stick to white pages black
with words. Pictures and notes
fail to answer enigmas.

Surrounded by darkness,
swims in data
as crabs in brackish water.

Illness thwarts her efforts,
strokes become shorter, slower,
breath labored. She swims alone
with images of love, of joy,
not yet free from her dilemmas.

Memories Fade
Bill Poppen

Fingers trace the jonquil petals,
fragile, translucent, color-rich.
Colors fade with breath
of wind jostling blossoms,
What colors have gone?

What's with the Poets?
Bill Poppen

Clump, drum, clump, drum.
They walk along Boder's ridge looking downward.
Boots kick pappus to the summer wind.

Before,
their hands had interlaced
like those of children skipping.

Now apart,
tears rest on eyelids,
pebbles of pain.

Tomorrow,
their busy pens will shed the hateful words
and rhymes of regret.

Yesterday's sheets of love verse,
will cram a wastebasket.
What's with the poets?

Their love has fallen
among the wilting buds.

Will the Chinese Elms Die?
Bill Poppen

It had better rain or the Chinese Elms
might die and nothing will remain
after this heat.

His boots kick up a cloud
of dry alfalfa leaves. He ponders
as he walks toward his tractor.
Counts-off the days
since they escaped the rain
under the Chinese Elm.
It's been twenty-four days
since he's seen her.
His grimy fingers fondle her photo.

They danced to *In the Mood* six years ago,
there had been plenty of rain.
He should have asked her then.

What if ...

Terri Verrette

what if, one day, a whole generation
awoke to a self-constructive
neurosis that pushed us through
the thin wail of the alarm clock
and opened our ears to the
deep gong that's sounded
from the moment the first human
woke to realize that nothing is forever
saying, life, your life, is short
spend it building and growing
and being something more than
the plumbing and frame of your house
the wiring and paint of your car
be more than a credit score
be the one to meet the need no one else sees
be self-constructive, release the power
that will change the way you live your life
into the ground

Self Expression
Terri Verrette

If you haven't seen me with my child
    you don't know me
if you haven't seen me at night
    dancing to the white light of a dream
    on the cold stone floor of my house
        you don't know me
if you haven't seen me shaken and tired
    crying blue brown stones at the base
    of a granite mountain
        you don't know me
but if you have heard me laugh
    you know something
if you have seen me cooking breakfast
    you know something
if you have read my careful prose
    you know something
if you have seen me cleaning house
    before my mother comes to visit
    you know something
I'm something else.

Beginning at the end
Terri Verrette

Some stories have their end written on the first page, you know the ones I'm talking about, from *Romeo and Juliet* down to *Bucket List* there've always been writers determined to test themselves against the hardest wall. I mean, how interesting can a story be when you know the ending before you've finished the first page? We readers don't fall for it often, the idea that how they get to the ending will be so deeply interesting that it's worth reading anyway. Romeo dead with Juliet's blood pooling around them both. Carter waiting in a coffee can on the side of Mount Everest for Edward's coffee can to be carried up. We nod our heads and go home. Why do we need to watch/read/hear any more?

From Shakespeare to Rob Reiner, I admire anyone with the guts to tell us the ending first. This dispenses with the smoke and mirrors lesser artists use to distract from their lesser stories. Oh, I like those stories too, the adventure of racing along into the unknown, unable to put it down because you just have to know how it ends. It's the ending that makes those books palatable, without that bit of mystery, "Oh, God, will Jake finally ask her to marry him after she's borne three of his children, forgiven his infidelity and perfidy, loved him through cancer ... and if he does will she have the self-respect to spit in his face?"

No, I admire most the writers who tell you up front, "she walked away" and then dare you to come along for the ride. Especially because very few who try that gambit have the talent to pull it off. So when she walked away, I recognized the moment for the pure high art it contained.

The day I met her she showed me how it would end. But something about the way she told the story kept me hooked. Through children, illness, good-times and bad it was there. I got so caught up in the story; I forgot I knew the final scene. Can you imagine? I just forgot. So there I was, drinking a glass of Red Bicycle Merlot, looking at the photo on the mantel. Twenty years younger, I was in love and she was beautiful. Only now I see that she was leaning away. I'd been so caught up in my dream; I lost sight of who she was. Or, maybe, she was such the artist that she'd obscured it under all the layers of drama and need. No matter who's dream, no matter what I thought I'd brought to the story, she walked out exactly the way she walked in. Awkward gait, cheap shoes, medium heel.

Respects
M. Merrill

What am I doing here?
I hope there's a bouquet
of photographs --
christenings, mortarboards
weddings
I need to connect.

Behind door number two
the funeral parlor trick
easier to view in soft light.

Centered in clots of guests,
darkly handsome sons stamped
with the high cheek-bones of Celtic warriors.
Daughters wear the same bones beneath
neat coiffures and composure, ferocity
strapped to their backs like broad-swords.

Friends offer pious platitudes
of eternal reward
colleagues remember cigars and
I'm just
one more
face
you can't place.

I offer an internet identity

Your eyes gather up my face
surprise silencing
that single trumpet note of grief.

We have laughed, shared,
Public insights, naked agonies,
mundane rasping of daily life;
felt each other's words.

(continued)

sorry
sounds
so
inadequate

Beneath your bemused gaze
I slide into the paralysis of
awkwardness,
grateful for the press of mourners
I step back into anonymity.

She Only Smokes on Tuesdays
Bill Poppen

Seduction floats on night mist,
fanned by words from cherry colored lips,
"I only smoke on Tuesdays."
Midnight striking.
"Take a drag on this exotic."
She waves the hard-flip box
like crack on a stick.
Two-toned browns pass from hand-to-hand
amid praises of their rich aroma.

Guess the flavor, becomes a contest —
match-struck flames of temptation burst forth.

Motorcycles on Cumberland Avenue roar,
college girls in hot pants and tees
encourage macho maneuvers.

Tasty tobacco imported from Malaysia
becomes the sin of choice.

Bananas and Coffee
Bill Poppen

Six thirty a.m. — cold feet
on the chilly kitchen floor. I run
water, fill the carafe.
I imagine Handel's *Water Music*
played by a streaming faucet.

Brown filters stick together.
Fingers tussle with a foil bag
of gourmet coffee — three, heck,
go with four tablespoons,
she might like her coffee strong today.
Two ceramic cups wait on the countertop.
Where is that half-and-half?

I flip the light switch,
yellow reflects to my eyes —
six bananas on a wire hanger.
I snap the biggest and brightest,
strip the peel as I climb the stairs.
Should I eat it all or share?

Warming next to her, I reach
for a small piece of banana,
place it to unsuspecting lips.
Her head turns, mouth half-open
as if expecting a kiss from a lover.
Her tender tongue reaches for the morsel,
soft moans whisper appreciation,
playfully rolls the tender fruit
across her palate — banana before coffee.

I envy that banana.

Will He Write About Me?
Bill Poppen

She heard that he's a poet
and wondered if he would write a poem
about her.

A wave of her hand, her hair,
shoulder length strands of pleasure,
would flag down any man.
She wondered if she had a poem
in her hair.

She spoke soft words
layered with one of those smiles
most guys adore
because it could mean "come closer"
or "not today." Ah, mystery!
Perhaps a poem rested
in her smile.

If she had cleavage!
Surely he would form lines about her,
compelled to tell the world
how she captured his lust.
She wished for a poem
in her cleavage.

She touched him.
He was open to her arm around his waist.
The poet felt like any other man.
She pressed closer.
Would he find a poem
in the warmth of her body?

Their legs entangled
unlike anything she could remember.
She wondered if there was a poem
hiding there.

(continued)

She wished she smoked,
noticed he did.
If they shared a cigarette,
he'd seem so *Hemingway*:
mysterious, open, alive,
someone she wished
she'd read for pleasure.

Maybe she should write a poem about him.

Rant Mama
Bill Poppen

She wears her anger
like a Pancho Villa gun belt.
Bloody leather straps
across her breasts. Her firebombs
awaken an old man
from his peaceful trance.

She haunts the hallways.
Those around her pray
she will find the path of peace.
Plead her to unlatch the cellar door
and drop her heavy weapons
down the stairwell to the basement.

New
Bill Poppen

Everything should be new.
She's fixed
and focused on his lips,
the sky, his wrinkled neck.

Love notes, mementoes
seldom on her table.
No talk of tomorrow,
no discourse of history,
for she might not notice
the texture of his hair.

Who cares about yesterday
or sins she's played.

She notices the wind, the rain,
his walk, his sway.
She might fall in love
with him again today.

Gallery Visit
Bill Poppen

She walks among the plates of beauty,
cast by hands, etched with details of passion,
molded with distortions of reality.

Sheets of art displayed for purchase
lay before her, behind her, beside her.
She steps, focuses one-by-one on colors —
glorious, dark, or blended
to capture heart. Seductive

textures tease
extending pleas from lithographs
silently begging to be carried
to a distant place.

They want her more
than she wants them.
She weighs her empty wallet,
tries to explain.

Looks for the door,
the exit to escape.

Infatuation
Bill Poppen

They drink
habit-forming
overdoses of love.

Kisses,
needle-sharp
piercing flesh.

Lust for that narcosis.

Weeding His Patch
M. Merrill

He had a pauper's funeral
county-paid space
near the mass grave
of floral tributes.

Natty and well-liked
back in the day,
He was knifed in his driveway.
Steel-toed boots
shattered orbits
spit teeth

a bullet pierced lung –

He should have struck his tent
wandered with the exodus –
(California, Carolina)

People who loved
his pacific kitchen table
where dense minds might
grasp tall words and imaginings

beyond grain elevators,
coke ovens,
Chevrolet.

Change he resisted
still weeding his patch
preaching sunrise
amid decay

and wolves who marked their territory.

The Poet Imagines A Happy Life
Terri Verrette

Oatmeal cookies with nuts and fruit
orange juice, champagne of truth
baby smiles, oil of the spirit of healing
not quite enough for big house on the hill
more than enough for laughter and still
it's the sound of your breath I'm remembering
more than the heartbeat deep in your chest
more than the way that you loved me your best
the sad little catch that presaged your death
it's the sound of your breath I'm remembering
not one day we spent is regretted or mourned
hours together led us to be borne
labor of love sweeps linoleum floors
past the hope of the life we once bargained for
it's the sound of your breath I'm remembering
when you touched me as though you remembered me well
from a lifetime before what a story you'd tell
to convince me that you were the one who rapelled
down the cliffs of destruction to hold me
it's the sound of your breath I'm remembering
aaaaaaaah, when a life has been spent in this way
unafraid of the moments spent harboring play
delaying the moment when you must away
beyond the reach of my fiercest embrace
who could say its been any part waste
when your breath in my memory still lingers.
it's the sound of your breath I'm remembering
it's the sound of your breath I'm remembering

Eulogy
M. Merrill

If asked
I will answer
Yes,

yes, I knew him

If pressed
I'll hesitate —

attempt invent

some detail

beyond barefoot days
bare-shouldered nights
untidy sheets.

His
favorite color
was
green.

Thief
M. Merrill

a breeze
handles the scribbles on my desk
there –
in the dust
your boot-prints.

Lunch
M. Merrill

Brown-bagged words,
a few light lines
melt in your eyes.

Sometimes
M. Merrill

like tomorrow
sometimes
does not come

a nebulous future
of half-baked dreams
dressed in a gown

and shoulders
that sparkle
with faery dust

laugh
but the truth is
we ache

for moments –
thinly veiled slices
of sometimes.

Extra
M Merrill

I want to fill a pitcher
with cooling
satisfaction; be
your drink of choice.

Can you see
it is not enough
for me to be
shipping peanuts

between

engagements?

No. I want to be
something –
the one
you crave

in the void of the night,
in your bones
immune to exorcism
at the bottom of a glass

I want to be
more
than
just extra.

Marking the Moment
Terri Verrette

Marriage dies in an unmarked moment.
One flesh walks in, lies down
two people rise and leave.
Shadows of connection follow
for days, weeks, or years as though
nothing has happened.

The favored of God know when spirit leaves.
Antony fainted with the musical procession
danced his Lord beyond Alexandra's gate.
Ezekiel saw the rise of glory from the temple
when Yawheh's spirit departed Jerusalem's wall.

For the ordinary, it comes as a slap
betrayal, sting of bitter words
occupation by hostile emotion
carting away our treasure in the night.
We cling to the hope of life.
But no one can span the gulf
when bone of bone is shattered.

Dare I?

Bill Poppen

I want you to melt into me,
slither around my body
like a cobra covets prey?

Dare I hope?

Strike me
with your venomous rapture,
your drips of passion.

How do I ask
you to wrap around
me again like yesterday?

Deja Who?
Terri Verrette

It didn't seem profound when I wrote the sentence. I was trying to go to sleep. Tired, but not tired enough. Old, but not old enough. Lying in the dark thinking back to when mama waited in the car while I went into the store for apples, milk, Campbell's soup, and sometimes for a treat
we could have bologna the kind with garlic and the red plastic strung around slices, ribbons to tie
and play string games. Although why I thought of that while I was trying to go to sleep, I couldn't say. But it wouldn't leave me, that silly little sentence about apples. So I pulled the notebook over, wrote it in the dark, and content with capture the words released me.

Until the next afternoon when I was shopping with my best friend, who turned from the MacIntosh, Fuji, Pink Lady, Jonathon, Granny Smith, Cameo, Gala display - brought the words out of the dark, out of the night off the page where they lay waiting, "When I was young, there were only three kinds of apples red, green, and yellow."

A Fool and Her Chocolate

Terri Verrette

Swing me a child-borne fantasy
 of probable stars and grass
  of chocolate milk cartons, big engines,
   of small pink flowers like nipples
dripping honey or darkness
 wrapped in a sky open blanket.

I want to be in as much as below
 and over before I get sour
  so fill me my oily bath
   bar me dark chocolate and pure
bubble me into your art of work
 serve me brandy with chile and cherries.
Blow me a boulder carved up
 of a generous cat and coffee
  of socks with stripes like tigers
   of the bed where geraniums grow
the day of my weeks with markers
 posing like hours of chocolate.

the way you looked
Kevin Urenda

the rawness of the truth
your eyes wore
the evening we first met
haunts my memory
like the ghosts of every Christmas
emotional pornographers
with a fetish for skin-tight desire
too painful
not to touch

tricks

Kevin Urenda

whispered in your ears
these words used to do
do circus tricks in your heart

no ordinary show
of danger and wonder
but something far more spectacular
often dangling my soul
on a fraying string
over a bottomless pit

sometimes falling
off the wire yourself
and letting me catch you
(I always loved that bit)

until the one day
your tent folded in on itself
and these words had to leave
the entertainment business
and find a new place to live

the kinks
Kevin Urenda

working out the kinks
is the last thing
I want to do
I love this pain
I want to work it
until it is raw
exposed
so far beyond
tender to the touch
that misery
is no longer a selfless act
of contrition
but a bauble
on an entire string
of horrors
pearls that even
the hungriest of swine would
refuse to swallow
jewels of unsurpassed
ugliness that I'll
only be convinced are
fit for me
when someone else
finally ignores them

that glitters
Kevin Urenda

he gathered
everything golden in his life
and cast ingots in the shape
of her eyes
molded exactly the way
she looked at him
when she wasn't quite sure
if she should feel happy
or not
he keeps them still
a shrine to the way she loved him
once

A Senior Kind of Rocking
Bill Poppen

Joy flowed from their eyes,
babies bouncing on teen-age knees
amid second-hand strollers.

Is happiness fraudulent?
Reflections may be hollow.
Had she confused stone with diamond?

Sitting now, babies gone,
photos covering age
marks along the wall,
She rocks at winter's dusk alone.
She hoped to have it all. I hear
sadness.

My Lost Earring
Terri Verrette

between pillows stacked and tumbled
arranged for poetry and chocolate
                              nothing
          but the memory of reading while you worked
          the sound of your keyboard, your pen

under the cushion of my chair
where we squeezed one more bedtime story
                              nothing
          but the memory of the baby
          whispering secrets in my ear

in all the quiet places made
resting grounds after a casual flip
                              nothing
          but the memory of a blue flash
          in an accidental mirror.

Order From My Menu
Terri Verrette

I've heard your stomach rumble, embarrassed
Laugh when rich sauce simmers.
You've been served food advertised, "just right"
Low fat, sugar free, high fiber, and vitamin enriched.
You accepted it with gratitude to the chef
and wondered what was wrong with you, unsatisfied.

I just want you to know, Baby.
I never learned to cook like that.

I learned in sulty southern kitchens
to serve cornbread with honey and milk for supper.
We dip fried chicken in thick white gravy (extra pepper)
Wash it down with sweet iced tea.
We have pecan pie after bar-be-que and
peach preserves with biscuits on the porch.

So you know what to expect
when you order from my menu.

I been thinking 'bout making a few changes
right below where it says, "Cold, cold beer
Cajun shrimp, (fresh outa the bayou, they are)"
Oh yeah, sure it's prepared the way you like
sautéed in garlic butter, seasoned with Tabasco.
Right there I'm putting a notice, you'll want to read.

You let me know, Baby, how hot can you stand it?

When it comes to a healthy appetite, seems to me anyway,
the most important thing is knowing
the customer is always right, and in my kitchen
you won't ever be surprised or embarrassed
'cause the food on your plate will be exactly
what you're hungry for.

Retired Lovers
Terri Verrette

He carries his chair out
to the morning sun,
she spreads the cape across his shoulders.
Scissors scrape through thin gray hair,
Rough and sure, despite the way
unsteady fingers linger at his nape.
They don't speak over distant traffic,
or the bird fussing at the squirrel
from the safety of a bush the old man pruned yesterday.
When she checks the sides, eyes meet,
they smile, his hand lifts
because she sways.
With the long tip of her comb,
she picks another lock, still damp,
with heat created after breakfast.
Wind lifts the snipped ends
blows them into the grass.
They have this chore to finish,
then lunch, then they plan a nap
with his arm draped across her stomach.

Upon Hearing Neruda Read Aloud
Terri Verrette

The candle caught my hair on fire
just before the poetry reading
driving shadows from the face
sharing deep voiced phrases
leaning close to whisper
words printed in pomegranate
drizzled across skin
lapped with cat tongue
between flickers, understandings
opening a burning dialogue.

oh mercy me
Terri Verrette

with the mercy of
your eyes your
voice you can
save me now
from the choice I'd make
if not for wine and you

see me here
I lounge across
the chair and drape
my comfortable
smile toward the sound
the words you speak

we could eat or
slip away and play
the games of
secret burning kisses
I'm just kidding
with my lightning eyes

so keep me here
and sing me the ring
to remind me the
way of the river
in its lonely bed
flowing smooth and deep

drink me the wine of chastity
and share me the bread
of love in we
the morning after a
night on town

with your fragrance
brought to mercy me.

Ballroom
Terri Verrette

"I don't dance," said the man
with his hand on my hip
"I've no rhythm, no grace
and my foot's prone to slip.
Look at me," he said looking
but not at my eyes.
He assumed I'd agree
no one danced when his size.

Bodies
move, touch, sway, sweat,
walk, bend, lift, turn, and
look back.
Slide into focus
and reach for the place
heat wavers like air
over pavement
in the desert.

"It's okay, you don't have to,"
I answered while swaying
"We'll stand here and share
just a moment of saying,
the things that we say only
when we are touching
outside of the words
that we're always rushing
to say one more time
before time has run out
with your hand on my hip
you won't have to …"

Step, forward, back
side, side, side
lean
and twist
say again
we can't dance.

(continued)

Turn my leg
raise my arm
quick skip in my belly, gasp
through fire writing a song
that slides like blue ink
down my spine.

Turn, slide, slide, slide
I'm me, no I'm you, no I'm
somewhere that there's never been
I before.

You don't have to dance
as long as you move

like

that.

Spoiled Damsel

Bill Poppen

Vases with flowers
must rest along walls or mantles.

Through morning sunlight,
she carries sharp scissors
poking from her apron pocket
back to hide behind tools
and bags of humus. Feet damp.

How he has changed,
his stem in a bottle
wilting in the morning dew
of July's sun.

Last Exit to Nameless
Bill Poppen

Sunset hues outline her scrub pine frame
leaning against the doorway.
Echoes bounce off walls, telling she's leaving.
Twice announces nameless destinations.

She's weary of empty Budweiser cans,
scattered *Field and Streams*,
unsigned anniversary cards.

Lukewarm beer swills over his tongue
like fingers gliding over a TV remote.

Lanterns flicker in solace.
Slamming door rocks the hallway walls.

Staying in the Game
Bill Poppen

Today she listens to her body—
the complexity churning beneath her skin,
the traces of passion bounding in her veins
as surging waves on the seashore.

She guides her hands creating something
of this moment — leaves indelible marks
to delight a student of nature.

Her breasts
are soft on the outside, roaring within.

Today her body
grows older,
moves slower.
She watches
her bones rise
slowly
to meet the day.

No bouncing flesh
comes with her
to face this day's
challenges.
She plays
the experience card
to stay alive
one more day.

Tea for Breakfast
Bill Poppen

Bored stiff, eyes cast upward,
she drifts by like fog rolling in from sea,
her body aching to absorb his wetness.

Newspapers clutter the breakfast nook,
his ink-stained fingers clutch ceramic
birthday cup — last year's surprise.

Today, the cup, the coffee, his only distractions.
The sweep of her garment grazes his back unnoticed.

She'll pour tea this morning and settle into her longings,
empty as her teacup.

Chivalry
Bill Poppen

I

Hospital chlorine, splash of lavender
mix with baby powder as she guards her newborn.

His fingers brush the fur on her collar,
while he helps her with the car door.

Wisps of spring
breeze through her auburn hair.

He captures her grace
soft as a red fox.

II

Shorter steps carry them
to and from their Taurus.

Hand-me-down walkers and bassinets
feel the weight of their grandchildren.

Welcome Guests stitched in black and red
greets overnighters in the nursery.

Seventy years old in her black shawl,
his hand cups her elbow, "Steady dear, steady."

The Ashram in Ashtabula
M. Merrill

Run away with me to the circus
I'll play the clown
and you shall be solemn.

The island-
that incongruous bridge, remember
I was lewd
you ran me down on the beach

Now's the time to stop dreaming
quit talking
build
the ashram in Ashtabula.

There'll never be a finer moment
than now
and you'll get to play
with my feet.

When Love Ends

Paulette Mauceri

I lay in the impression
your body made in our bed
and wonder how long
the pillow will remain warm.

Silence makes me hear you more,
the dark weight of the hours
drag behind me
as I pray to an altar
built on the edge of my despair.

A mad woman staring into her secrets,
I reach for you through the shadows,
a hope junkie.

I cling to the taste of your body
a river I still yearn to drink
the slam of the door no louder
than the infinite sound of alone.

Beg of Night
Paulette Mauceri

Alone in the night she marries
the dark curve of memory
behind her eyes
secreting regrets.

She parts brambles in the shadows
where skeletons ride bicycles
whispering with voices flat and cold
like the side of a knife.

She struggles to keep from unraveling,
hopes joy will look out the window
to let her in.

She remembers the good like a drunkard forgets,
the dream never rescues the maiden,
her fate like loose quicksilver
on a nest of cracks.

Godless Libertine
Paulette Mauceri

The devil came to him this morning,
a costumed courtesan laying
her body on the dark side of his soul.

Like a carrion crow,
he hungered for sacrifice,
touched by the spirit of lost hope.

Seeking nirvana, though his bed, filled
with the rich scent of perfume,
bathes him in deceit.

One final act of degradation, his intermezzo,
folds of the pillow fashioning a ladder
out of regret.

Indian Summer
Beth Anne Cox

Summer. How I love it, as I
Walk to the mailbox; a hot
Breeze ripples gauzy flounces,
And dust sneaks under my toes.
Indian summer, they call it.
Everything around me shimmers
In a golden haze, and
The leaves are still green.
Across the road, glossy stalks
Bow beneath their swollen weight.
Silken floss is toasted brown
And the corn so filled with rich milk
I can smell its sweetness.

Summer. How I love it.

The beast roars into the field
Voracious, cacophonous,
Crushing and devouring all of summer
In a matter of greedy moments.
The ground becomes littered with
Chewed husks and undigested
Stalks, bereft of the harvest
So proudly borne. The bounty
Now nothing so much as
Picnic trash, whirling around
My feet. I am stunned.

In that instant, I see
The golden haze is
Now a tumble of pumpkins
For sale. And the leaves, so green
A moment before, are actually
Hemstitched all around with
Amber, bronze, copper, crimson,
Gold, persimmon, pomegranate and quince.

I see autumn arrive.

Hydrotherapy

Beth Anne Cox

Nerves jangling,
knees trembling,
I stepped
into the bath.
Hotter than you liked it,
you stepped in, too.
Rarely wary, but that night
you were.

Surrounded by
elemental warmth
and swirling, silken
motion, we
melted.
I kissed you first...
does it matter?

Out of the bath, now
quivering, shivering
for a wholly, holy
different reason.
Water
dripping, beading,
slickened quicksilver;
Surrounded by
your arms
your lips
your eyes.

(continued)

The softness of
slow moving, quiet
waves, gently
lapping.
The fierceness of
insistent, demanding
waves; a tide
not to be denied.
Sweat.
Tears.
Limbs loosening,
languorously liquid,
entwined on
this sugar beach.

Light Tracings
Sandra Erickson

Dappled rays
reach beyond backlit clouds,
an unexpected irridescence
glitters afternoon chimes,

slides down summer leaves
scattered rustling
across orchard grass,
bees humming up and up and up;

long winded ribbons
shadow wildflowers,
wander along the edges
of the water seller's song,

hopscotch river rocks
and flat blue stones,
step over cats napping
on summer brick;

silent warmth welcomes
diaphanous shutterings
at screened windows
and open doors,

pours onto puddled floors,
weaving patterned threads,
warp and weft
into kilim colors;

now, breathless, sleeping close,
spooned arm comforts your waist,
gingerly fingers your hair
and kisses your golden skin;

(continued)

I follow the same path,
tracing lightly.

from Epiphany 47, Winner of Shadow Poetry's 3rd Biannual Chapbook
Competition and featured works in Shadows of the Season and Shadows Ink
Chapbook: Series 2, Volume 3.

Anti-Gravitational Pull
Sandra Erickson

Only your smile holds the sun aloft,
only your light touch
transcends the stars and moon,

rising and setting
as the universe revolves
into those dark spaces between us.

Smile, I will shine for you,
touch, and my circle dance
illuminates every shadowed peripheries,

all disquietude, eclipsed,
and the weighted world suspended
from the apex of our laughter.

first published in Dances with Love, by Michael Ernest Sweet/2005

Airborne

Sandra Erickson

Perched along hard edges,
of theoretical flight,
the wings of birds,
and breath of angels.

Forgive me the wind
when levity fails,
I remember too well
gravity's embrace -

dead weight,
heavy landings,
one foot in the grave;
my feathered soul escapes.

from Epiphany 47, Winner of Shadow Poetry's 3rd Biannual Chapbook Competition and featured works in Shadows of the Season and Shadows Ink Chapbook: Series 2, Volume 3. ; Lulu publications and Michael Sweet publications in association with Learning for a Cause/2008

About the Poets:

Beth Anne Cox is a poet, writer, wife, mother, daughter, sister and friend. She lives on an island with her husband, Gerald, and daughter Elizabeth. She is most often found in front of the fire reading, at her desk writing, or in the library where she works among--you guessed it--books. Beth Anne has published columns in *The Goshen News*, *The Variety Press*, and the *Times-Union*. Her work may also be viewed at http://www.xanga.com/GracieBC, at http://www.GotPoetry.com, and at http://www.ElizabethVirdon.com.

Poet and potter, **Sandra Erickson** lives in Vermont where she divides her time between the studio, her computer and her granddaughter. Sandra was recently published in the University of Maine's *Binnacle*, her second book of poetry *Airborne* was released in December 2008.

Marge Merrill, published writer and host of *The Screening Room*, a spoken word venue in Western New York; released her first CD, eclectic, in 2005. Currently, she is working on her next spoken word collection of poetry and a chapbook. Visit her at: http://www.wordfaery.com/. Her poems *Weeding His Patch* and *Eulogy* were previously published in *Beyond Bones* a collection of poetry featuring writers from Western New York. Volume 1 Fall 2009 D. H. May Fair Publishing.

Orphaned before she was born in 1965, **Sarah Sydney Nash's** favorite book as a child was *Are You My Mother?* Even at the tender age of five, she could argue with any adult that the author of this book wasn't Dr. Seuss, and so her editorial skills were finely honed; which is why she is the production editor for The *Hiss Quarterly*. Ms. Nash has managed to publish short stories, articles, commentary and poetry all over the place. Someday she will finish writing many of the books she's started; and will submit most of the poetry she has scribbled on the backs of envelopes and deposit slips (who uses those anyway?). She's in love with the same guy she's been in love with since she was eight, still lives with her three adult children and will probably live in West Coast Washington someday.

William A. Poppen is retired and spends most of his time writing poetry, taking photographs, hiking, biking and traveling with his wife, Yvonne. His photos have been published on-line in The *Hiss Quarterly* and poems have appeared on-line in *Chanterelle's Notebook*, *The Cat's Meow for Writers &*

Readers, and *Symbiotic Poetry*. Written works have been in *The Creative Writer*, 2008, *GotPoetry Anthology* and *New Millennium Writings* (2007-08).

Mary Elizabeth Thompson is a writer, artist, and naturalist living in Northern Virginia. Her poetry draws on her dark inner shadows and her art attempts to capture the world as she sees it. When she's not hiking or birding, she's journaling, reading, or cuddled up in front of the TV with her husband of 27 years and her two dogs.

Engineer-designer **Kevin Urenda** brings to poetry a love of precision that enables him to craft words into tight little gems that tell multiple stories. He focuses on the edges of life, beginnings and endings, surprises and realizations because it's when you're at the edge of the horizon that the light makes its most spectacular display.

Terri Verrette is a published author of short stories, book reviews, poetry, articles, and opinion/editorial work. She was born in Arkansas, and moved through seven other states before landing in the high desert of the southwest which she loves and plans never to leave. She is presently (always) working on a novel in between raising her sons and working in a bank.

Dan Tharp is author of 3 chapbooks: *Side by Side, Yielding Desire to Fate* and *A Season Made for Wandering* published through Shadowpoetry.com. http://www.shadowpoetry.com/members/hollowquilltrail/277/dantharp. html   Dan also has a book of poetry, *A Rose in the Briar* due to be published late Spring, 2009 through Poetic Matrix Press.

Paulette Mauceri is a published writer of fiction, non-fiction, poetry, as well as a research consultant for special interest. She is about to launch her first novel, *Desert Bones*, a fictional murder mystery set in the southwest. Paulette lives in the foothills of the beautiful Nevada desert.